The Roman Empire i

by W. E. Vine

PREFACE.

The following pages are the outcome of several conversations with inquirers shortly after the outbreak of the great war, in 1914, and of requests for notes of the views expressed. The subject of these conversations had occupied the earnest if intermittent attention of the writer for over twenty years. The notes were expanded into a series of articles which appeared in The Witness during 1915. These have been revised and somewhat extended for the present volume, especially the last chapter, much of which was previously precluded by limitations of space.

In regard to past history, the outlines of events connected with the Roman and Turkish Empires are given with the hope that the records will prove helpful to those who read the history of Nations in the light of Scripture.

In regard to the future, while there are many events which the Word of God has foretold with absolute clearness, and upon these we may speak unreservedly, yet there are many circumstances concerning which definite prediction has been designedly withheld, and upon which prophecy is therefore obscure. In such matters an effort has been made to avoid dogmatism. Prophecy was not given in order for us to prophesy.

On the other hand, the prophetic Scriptures are not to be neglected. Difficulty in understanding them is no reason for disregarding them. They are part of that Word, the whole of which is declared to be "profitable for doctrine, for reproof, for correction, for instruction in righteousness" (2 Tim. 3. 16). They therefore demand prayerful and patient meditation.

For a speaker to refer to the study of the prophecies in a way which tends to minimise their importance in the minds of his hearers is to dishonour both the sacred Word and Him who inspired it. It is significant that the book of the Revelation opens with a promise of blessing to him who reads (the reference is especially to public reading) and to those who "hear the words of the prophecy, and keep the things which are written therein" (chap. 1. 3), and at the close repeats the blessing for him who keeps its words (chap. 22. 7).

The quotations in the present volume are from the Revised Version, the comparatively greater accuracy of its translations being important for a correct understanding of many of the passages considered.

While the book is published at the request of several friends, the author fulfils such request with the earnest desire that in matters of doctrine that only may be accepted which can be confirmed from the Word of God itself, and that the Lord may graciously own what is in accordance with His mind for the glory of His Name and the profit of the reader.

BATH, 1916. W. E. VINE.

CHAPTER I.

THE TIMES OF THE GENTILES.

The overthrow of the kingdom of Judah recorded in 2 Kings 24 and 25, and in the opening words of the book of Daniel, was a remarkable crisis in the history of the world. In judgment upon the people of God for their long-continued iniquity, sovereignty was removed from their hands, king and people were led into captivity, and Jerusalem was, in fulfilment of Jeremiah's words, given into the hand of Nebuchadnezzar, the king of Babylon (Jer. 21. 10). The government of their land was thus committed to the Gentiles, and with the Gentiles it has remained from that day till now. These events took place in 606 and 587 B.C.

The Times of the Gentiles.

But Gentile control is not to continue indefinitely. This, which is plain from many Scriptures, was intimated by Christ to His disciples when He said of Jerusalem that the city would "be trodden down of the Gentiles until the times of the Gentiles be fulfilled" (Luke 21. 24). The phrase, "the times of the

Gentiles," calls for consideration, and especially as it has to do with Nebuchadnezzar's conquest just mentioned.

There are two words translated "times" in the New Testament; one is chronoi, which is invariably rendered "times;" the other is kairoi, which, when the two are found together, is rendered "seasons." Thus Paul, in writing to the Thessalonian Church, says, "But concerning the times and the seasons, brethren, ye have no need that aught be written unto you" (1 Thess. 5. 1, R.V.; cp. Acts 1.7). We may distinguish "seasons" from "times" in the following way: "times" denotes mere duration, lengths of time; "seasons" implies that these lengths of time have certain events or circumstances associated with them by which they are characterised. Thus the words almost exactly correspond to the terms "periods" and "epochs." Now the word kairoi, "seasons," is used in the phrase translated "the times of the Gentiles," which might accordingly be rendered "the seasons of the Gentiles." We look, then, for some special characteristic of the period or periods thus designated. We have observed that Nebuchadnezzar's overthrow of the kingdom of Judah involved the transference of its sovereignty from Jew to Gentile from that event onward. "The times of the Gentiles," accordingly, is that period, or succession of periods, during which dominion over the Jews and their land is committed to Gentile Powers.

Nebuchadnezzar's Dream.

Special significance attaches to the fact that no sooner had the times of the Gentiles begun than God made known the future course of their authority over His people, and the character and doom of that authority, and made it known to the first Gentile conqueror himself. It was in the second year of his reign that Nebuchadnezzar saw in a dream the great image by means of which the purposes of God were to be communicated to him. The description of this, given by Daniel to the troubled monarch, is as follows: "Thou, O king, sawest, and behold a great image. This image, which was mighty, and whose brightness was excellent, stood before thee; and the aspect thereof was terrible. As for this image, his head was of fine gold, his breast and his arms of silver, his belly and his thighs of brass, his legs of iron, his feet part of iron, and part of clay. Thou sawest till that a stone was cut out without hands, which smote the image upon his feet that were of iron and clay, and brake them in pieces. Then was the iron, the clay, the brass, the silver, and the gold, broken in pieces together, and became like the chaff of the summer threshing-floors: and the wind carried them away, that no place was found for them: and the stone that smote the image became a great mountain, and filled the whole earth" (Dan. 2. 31-35).

Interpreting this vision, the prophet identified Nebuchadnezzar, the Chaldean monarch, with the head of gold, and foretold that his kingdom, or empire, would be followed in succession by three others, corresponding respectively to the different parts of the remainder of the image and to the nature of the metals composing them. Of the four kingdoms the last is to engage our chief attention in these papers. Passing from the first, the =Chaldean=, as specified in Daniel's words to the king, "Thou art this head of gold" (v. 38), we are shown that the second kingdom was that of the =Medes and Persians= by the prophet's record of the doom of Nebuchadnezzar's successor, Belshazzar: "In that night Belshazzar the Chaldean king was slain. And Darius the Mede received the kingdom" (Dan. 5. 30, 31; cp. v. 28). That the third kingdom was the =Grecian= we find in the interpretation of part of a vision recorded in the eighth chapter: "The ram which thou sawest that had the two horns, they are the kings of Media and Persia. And the rough he-goat [who was seen to destroy the ram, v. 8] is the king of Greece" (vv. 20, 21; cp. chap. 10. 20).

The Fourth Kingdom.

The name of the fourth kingdom is not mentioned in the Old Testament, but the prediction given in the ninth chapter of Daniel's prophecies sufficiently identifies it. Messiah, it was said, would be cut off, and the people of a coming prince would destroy the city and the sanctuary. Now we know that the perpetrators of this were the Romans. We know, too, that by them the Grecian empire was conquered. The world-wide rule of the first =Roman= Emperor is indicated in the words of Luke's introduction to his record of the birth of Christ:

"Now it came to pass in those days, there went out a decree from Caesar Augustus, that all the world should be enrolled" (Luke 2. 1).

It is important to note that this fourth kingdom will, in its final condition, be in world-wide authority at the close of the times of the Gentiles, that is, that the Roman power, though in a divided state, will not be finally destroyed until it meets its doom at the hands of the Son of God. This fact, which will receive fuller treatment later, and is borne out by several Scriptures, is plainly indicated in the passage which describes the last state of the fourth kingdom and its destruction. Immediately after showing that it would be a divided kingdom, and describing the nature of that division (vv. 41-43), the prophet says: "And in the days of those kings shall the God of Heaven set up a kingdom, which shall never be destroyed, nor shall the sovereignty thereof be left to another people; but it shall break in pieces and consume all these kingdoms, and it shall stand for ever" (v. 44). Now this indestructible kingdom cannot be other than that of Christ, and by His kingdom the fourth is to be broken in pieces and consumed, thus involving the overthrow of all forms of Gentile authority. Obviously no form of world government will exist between that of the fourth kingdom, in its condition described in verses 42, 43, and the kingdom of Christ which destroys it.

CHAPTER II.

THE ROMAN DOMINION.

An understanding of the Scriptures does not depend upon access to other books, or reference to historical records outside the limits of the Bible. The Word of God is its own interpreter, and all that is needed for our establishment in the faith is contained in its pages. On the other hand, the Bible throws light upon history not recorded therein, and it is with that in view that we give certain historical outlines in dealing with our subject.

The first part of the prophet's description of the fourth kingdom is as follows: "The fourth kingdom shall be strong as iron: forasmuch as iron breaketh in pieces and subdueth all things: and as iron that crusheth all these, shall it break in pieces and crush" (v. 40). A similar description is given in his account of a subsequent vision, in which he saw four great beasts coming up from the sea. In this vision the Roman kingdom again was undoubtedly symbolised by the fourth beast. This beast he describes as "terrible and powerful, and strong exceedingly; and it had great iron teeth: it devoured and brake in pieces, and stamped the residue with his feet" (7. 7). So, again, in the words of the interpretation: "The fourth beast shall be a fourth kingdom upon earth, which shall be diverse from all the kingdoms, and shall devour the whole earth, and shall tread it down, and break it in pieces" (v. 23). Now all this exactly depicts the Roman power in its subjugation and control of the nations which eventually composed its empire. In the light, then, of these prophecies we give a brief sketch of its rise and conquests.

The Rise and Progress of the Roman Empire.

The Romans, who early in the third century B.C. had become masters of all Italy, save in the extreme north, were drawn into a course of conquest beyond the limits of their own country by the rivalry of the rapidly advancing power of Carthage in North Africa. Carthage, a city founded some centuries earlier by Phoenician colonists from Tyre and Sidon, had at length become the capital of a great North African empire, stretching from Tripoli to the Atlantic Ocean, and embracing settlements elsewhere in countries and islands of the Mediterranean. These settlements included the greater part of Sicily, and that island, situated between the rival nations, became the first bone of contention between them. The precise cause of the struggle must not occupy us here, but the circumstances which decided the Roman Government, in 264 B.C., upon an invasion of Sicily were of the deepest significance in the history of the world. By the year 242 Sicily was subdued. In the following year the island was ceded by Carthage, and the extension of Roman dominion beyond Italy was begun. The war continued intermittently, with many vicissitudes, for a century, but eventually the Carthagians were overwhelmingly defeated by land and sea. "Think you that Carthage or that Rome will be content, after the victory, with its own country and Sicily?" said a Greek orator, while the issues of the struggle in its earliest stage were yet in the balance. Rome's vast ambition, and her abundant means of gratifying it, justified the orator's fears. The islands of Sardinia and Corsica were shortly afterwards seized.

Defeated in Sicily, Carthage extended her dominions in Spain and made that country a base for marching through Gaul to attack the Romans from the north. Though their renowned leader Hannibal met with success, their effort was doomed to failure. Meanwhile Roman armies had pushed into Spain. After a fierce struggle of thirteen years the Carthagians were completely overcome there, and Spain soon became a Roman province. By the decisive battle of Zama, in North Africa, in 202, Carthage and its territories became tributary, and thus all the western Mediterranean passed under the supremacy of Rome. Eventually in 146, as a result of a final war, Carthage was razed to the ground, and its North African kingdom was constituted a Roman province under the name of Africa. War with the Celts in North Italy, commencing the next year, resulted in the extension of the boundary to the Alps, and countries beyond began to feel the terror of the Roman name.

Eastward Extension.

The second century B.C. witnessed the spread of the iron rule eastward. The Grecian Empire of Alexander the Great, the third mentioned in Daniel's interpretation, had embraced all the countries surrounding the eastern half of the Mediterranean and had stretched far beyond the Euphrates. The disintegration of Alexander's empire after his death prepared the way for the Romans. Macedonia, the former seat of that empire, was their first great objective. A pretext for war was soon forthcoming, and war was actually declared in 200 B.C. A series of struggles ensued, and Macedonia was not finally subdued for over thirty years. Meanwhile matters had developed in Greece and Asia Minor. In the latter country Antiochus III., the Great, who had also conquered Syria and Palestine, was seeking to extend his dominions. Cities and states of Asia Minor, however, groaning under the tyranny of Antiochus, appealed to Rome for aid. The Romans declared war against him in 192 B.C. The first conflict occurred in Greece, which was largely under his influence. An early victory secured the submission of the Greek states. Antiochus retreated into Asia Minor, and was finally crushed at Magnesia in 190. The whole of Asia Minor was then surrendered to Rome. Actual possession was postponed and local government was largely granted both there and in Greece. But that policy proved impracticable, and the force of circumstances compelled a forward movement to universal empire. There was no such thing as the balance of power in the ancient world. Once a country became predominant there was nothing for it but the subjugation of its neighbours. The extension of Rome's dominions eastward was a fulfilment of a destiny beyond its own control. The reverent student of Scripture sees in the course of these events the unfolding of God's plans and the fulfilment of His Word.

The final campaign against the Macedonians was opened in 169 B.C., and in the next year they were overwhelmed at the decisive battle of Pydna. Macedonia and the adjacent state of Illyria became tributary, and eventually were reduced to Roman provinces.

The Romans then felt the necessity of definitely annexing Greece. Seventy towns in that country were plundered and 150,000 inhabitants were sold into slavery. Antiochus IV., Epiphanes, was now king of Syria and Palestine, and had possessed himself of almost the whole of Egypt. Such was the effect of the battle of Pydna, however, that he was at once compelled to hand over Egypt to the conquerors, and that country became a Roman protectorate. Syria passed under Roman control at the death of Antiochus Epiphanes, in 164, and by the end of a few decades all the states of Asia Minor had been incorporated.

Thus by the middle of this century the Republic of Rome had gained ascendancy east and west. Its senate was recognised by the civilised world as "the supreme tribunal for kings and nations." Early in the next century Dalmatia and Thrace were subdued, and the latter was incorporated in the province of Macedonia. Wars with Mithradates, King of Pontus, Cappadocia and Armenia, resulted in the conquest of all his territories, and provinces were formed out of the states from thence westward to the 灾 ean sea.

Palestine Annexed.

This century saw the actual interference of Rome in the affairs of Judea. Syria had been made a province in 65 B.C. by the Roman General Pompey, and from thence he intervened in a strife which had for some time been raging amongst the leaders of the Jews. In 63 he marched an army into Judea and took Jerusalem. At the final assault upon the Temple 12,000 Jews perished. Judea thus passed under the iron heel.

As a result of the wars of Caesar in north-western Europe, in 58-51 B.C., what are now Switzerland, France, and Belgium were subdued and Britain was invaded. By C 鉦 ar also Roman authority in Africa was consolidated across the entire length of the north of the continent. The conquests of Rome as a Republic were complete. The Mediterranean had become a "Roman lake."

[Illustration: THE ROMAN EMPIRE IN APOSTOLIC TIMES.]

The Empire Completed.

In 27 B.C. the purely Republican form of constitution was abolished, and the government of the Roman world was concentrated in the hands of an Emperor, the C 鉦 ar Augustus of Luke 2.1. In his reign were fulfilled the prophecies foretelling the Birth of Christ. When the Prince of Peace was born in Bethlehem the din of strife was hushed throughout the empire, and Rome, under the restraining hand of God, ceased for a time its warring. By Augustus the northern territories of the empire were extended to practically the entire length of the Danube. The greater part of Britain became a province under Claudius. A later Emperor, Trajan, added, at the beginning of the second century A.D., the province of Dacia, covering what are now Transylvania and most of Roumania. Under Marcus Aurelius (161-180) a large part of Mesopotamia was finally annexed.

This completes the actual conquests of the Romans. We will now note certain characteristics of their method of subjugation, viewed in the light of Daniel's prophecy concerning the fourth kingdom, that, like iron, it would "break in pieces and crush."

The Crushing of the Nations.

The crushing process was evidenced in many ways, and especially by the establishment of a general system of slavery, which almost everywhere supplanted free labour. Slave-hunting and slave-dealing became a profession. To such an extent were they carried on at one period that certain provinces were well nigh depopulated. We are told that at the great slave-market in the island of Delos, off Greece, as many as ten thousand slaves were disembarked in the morning and bought up before the evening of the same day. Chained gangs worked under overseers and were confined in prison at night. To take an instance of the extreme rigour of the laws regulating the traffic, it is recorded by the historian Tacitus, that once, when the Prefect of Rome had been killed by one of his slaves, of whom he owned a vast number, the whole of his slaves, many of them women and children, were executed together, in accordance with an ancient law. That event took place about the time, apparently, at which the Apostle Paul arrived at Rome.

But not only were the nations ground down by slavery, the pages of Roman history abound in records of wholesale massacre and butchery. We may note, for instance, Luke's statement of Pilate's slaughter of Galil鎔ns while they were sacrificing (Luke 13. 1). Records abound, too, of grossly burdensome taxation and financial exactions, in which the Romans outdid all tyrants that had preceded them. Usury flourished in the last century as it had never done before. Four per cent. per month was an ordinary exaction for a loan to a community. On one occasion a Roman banker, who had a claim on the municipality of Salamis, in Cyprus, kept its council blockaded until five of its members died of hunger.

By these methods the provinces of the empire were at one period reduced to a condition of unsurpassed misery. Nothing could more vividly describe the course of such a kingdom and the control exercised by it than the words of Daniel quoted above.

The Twofold Division.

This fourth kingdom was destined to be divided; and in two respects, territorial and constitutional. The territorial division was indicated by the symbolism of the legs and feet of the image of Nebuchadnezzar's vision; the constitutional division was declared in Daniel's interpretation concerning the iron and clay (v. 40). The former of these divisions claims our consideration first. Territorially the kingdom would be first divided into two parts corresponding with the legs of the image. This actually took place in the fourth century of the present era.

The Roman Empire had continued in a more or less united condition for over three centuries after the accession of its first Emperor, Augustus, in 27 B.C., though various signs of a coming division manifested themselves. It was not unusual, for instance, for an emperor to appoint an associate with himself in the imperial rank, and on one occasion Maximian, who thus became associated with Diocletian in A.D. 288, actually established his seat of government at Nicomedia, in Asia Minor. Constantine (323-337) united the empire under his sole rule, but paved the way for the final separation of east from west by founding, in 328, the city of Constantinople as a second Rome, after his own name, and establishing it as an eastern centre of government with its own legislative institutions. This arrangement was favoured by several conditions, national and otherwise, which characterised the countries of the eastern half as distinct from those of the western.

At the death of Constantine, in 337, his dominions were divided among his three sons, a division, however, which lasted but a brief time. The empire was in 353 again united under Constantius, the survivor of the three. The long impending division into two parts took place under Valentinian I., in the year of his accession, 364. Yielding to the wish of his soldiers that he should associate a colleague with himself, he placed his brother Valens in power in the east, with headquarters at Constantinople, he himself retaining control over the west.

The Tenfold Division.

Prophetic Scriptures show that the Roman Empire would be further divided. Now while the ten toes of the image in Nebuchadnezzar's dream have not improperly been regarded as indicative of a tenfold division, the fact that the image had ten toes would be insufficient of itself to signify this, for the toes are naturally essential to a complete human figure. Moreover, the hands and their fingers, equally essential parts, have no territorial significance attached to them. The conclusion regarding the toes is, however, justified when we find the tenfold division abundantly confirmed by other Scriptures.

Thus the fourth beast in the vision in chapter 7, which, as we have seen, likewise symbolised the Roman kingdom, is described as having ten horns (v. 7). The interpretation clearly tells us what these are: "And as for the ten horns, out of the kingdom (the fourth) shall ten kings arise" (v. 24). The Apocalypse gives us further information regarding this division, unfolding with increasing clearness the details connected with it. In one of the visions given to the apostle John, he sees "a great red dragon, having seven heads and ten horns" (Rev. 12. 3). The meaning of the ten horns is not there explained. We are told that the great dragon is "the old serpent, he that is called the Devil and Satan, the deceiver of the whole world" (v. 9). Turning now to the next chapter, we find another vision recorded, giving a fresh view of the same subject. A beast was seen "coming up out of the sea, having ten horns and seven heads, and on his horns ten diadems, and upon his heads names of blasphemy" (chap. 13. 1). Again an explanation of the ten horns is withheld, but that they are identical with those of the twelfth chapter is undeniable. The Apostle receives, however, a further vision, recorded in chapter 17: "I saw a woman sitting upon a scarlet-coloured beast, full of names of blasphemy, having seven heads and ten horns" (chap. 17. 3). And now the symbolism of the horns is explained: "the ten horns that thou sawest are ten kings, which have received no kingdom as yet; but they receive authority as kings, with the beast, for one hour. These have one mind, and they give their power and authority unto the beast" (vv. 12, 13).

We are now concerned, of course, solely with the tenfold division of the empire; other details of the visions just referred to remain for later consideration. We cannot fail to see that what is symbolised by the ten toes of the image, and by the ten horns of the fourth beast as revealed to Daniel, is identical with what is symbolised by the ten horns of the dragon and of the beast seen by John, namely, the Roman kingdom in its ultimately divided condition.

A Comparison of the Visions.

The following points are noteworthy in comparing these visions relatively to the tenfold division. First, there is a parallelism in the order of the revelations given to the two seers, Daniel and John. A preliminary vision is given to each--more than one in the case of John--in which, in the matter of this territorial partition, symbols occur without explanation. Each then receives a further vision, in the interpretation of which the eventual division into ten kingdoms is plainly disclosed. To Daniel it is said: "As for the ten horns, out of the kingdom shall ten kings arise;" and to John: "The ten horns that thou sawest are ten kings, ... which receive authority as kings with the beast for one hour."

Second, the ten kingdoms are seen to be contemporaneous, as is indicated by the co-existence of the ten horns of the beast, and further, by the fact that the ten kings mutually agree to a certain line of policy in handing over their authority to a supreme potentate (Rev. 17. 12, 13).

Third, it is evident that the fourth kingdom is the last of the Gentile world-powers, and that it will exist in its tenfold state at the end of the times of the Gentiles. We observed this above in the case of the image, from the fact that the stone, symbolising the kingdom of Christ, smote the image upon its toes. So now, in the vision of the four beasts, it is the fourth beast that is slain, his body destroyed, and given to be burned (Dan. 7. 11). The Personal Agent of this destruction is here made known: "I saw in the night visions, and, behold, there came with the clouds of Heaven One like unto a son of man, and He came even to the Ancient of Days, ... and there was given Him dominion, and glory, and a kingdom, that all the peoples, nations, and languages should serve Him: His dominion is an everlasting dominion, which shall not pass away, and His kingdom that which shall not be destroyed" (vv. 13, 14). The finality of the fourth kingdom is clearer still from the interpretation given in the remainder of the chapter. The final world-ruler is, of course, prominent in this vision; in his destruction is involved the destruction of his kingdom; his power and aggression are terminated when the Ancient of Days comes (v. 22); then it is that "the judgment shall sit, and they shall take away his dominion, to consume and to destroy it unto the end. And the kingdom and the dominion, and the greatness of the kingdoms under the whole heaven, shall be given to the people of the saints of the Most High: His kingdom is an everlasting kingdom, and all dominions shall serve and obey Him" (vv. 26, 27). Similarly, again, in Revelation 13 and 17, in the corresponding visions of the beast and its ten horns, the ten kings and their federal head, ruling at the time of the end, "shall war against the Lamb, and the Lamb shall overcome them, for He is Lord of lords, and King of kings; and they also shall overcome that are with Him, called and chosen and faithful" (Rev. 17. 14).

The crushing of the image by the stone, the slaying of the fourth beast before the Ancient of Days, and the conquest of the ten kings and their chief by the Lamb, are therefore different views of the same event. The tenfold division of the fourth kingdom is obviously still future, and marks the condition of the world-government at the close of the times of the Gentiles, and immediately prior to the kingdom of Christ.

The Testimony of Early Christian Writers.

That the Roman Empire would in its final form be divided into ten kingdoms was held by Christian writers of the earliest post-apostolic times. Their opinions are here given, not as forming any basis of exposition, but as expressions of early Christian conception of the Scriptures under consideration.

What is known as "The Epistle of Barnabas," probably written early in the second century A.D., quotes from Daniel concerning the ten kingdoms to show that they would exist at the consummation of the present age. Irenes (circa A.D. 120-202), a disciple of Polycarp, who had been a companion of the apostle John, observes that "the ten toes are ten kings, among whom the kingdom will be divided." Tertullian, a contemporary of Irenes, remarks that "the disintegration and dispersion of the Roman State among the ten kings will produce Antichrist, and then shall be revealed that Wicked One, whom the Lord Jesus shall slay with the breath of His mouth and destroy by the brightness of His manifestation." Hippolytus, who was a follower of Irenes, and flourished in the first half of the third century, makes similar reference to the ultimate division. Lactantius, of the latter half of the third and the early part of the fourth centuries, writes as follows: "The Empire will be sub-divided, and the powers of government, after being frittered away and shared among many, will be undermined. Civil discords will then ensue, nor will there be respite from destructive wars, until ten kings arise at once, who will divide the world among themselves to consume rather than to govern it." Cyril (circa 315-386), who became bishop of Jerusalem in 350, quoting from Daniel, and speaking of the Empire and its future division, implies that teaching on the subject was customary in the churches. Jerome (342-420) observes that "at the end of the world, when the kingdom of the Romans is to be destroyed, there will be ten kings to divide the Roman world among themselves." Similarly writes Theodoret in the fifth century, and others of that time make more or less direct reference to the subject. While the views of these writers differ considerably on other points of detail, all are unanimous as to the eventual division of the Empire among ten contemporaneous potentates.

Processes at Work Since the Twofold Division.

The medieval and modern history of the lands originally constituting the Roman Empire is a history of the formation of independent states in such a way as to point to the eventual revival of the Empire in the tenfold division we have been considering. The process has been a long and involved one, for the counsels of God have had a far wider range than the mere shaping of national destiny. It has been the Divine pleasure, for instance, that the Gospel should be spread among all nations for the purpose of taking out from among them a people for the Name of Christ, and for the formation thereby of His Church. In contradistinction to this, and from the standpoint of the world itself, which, though under God's control, remains in alienation from Him, there has been a gradual development of the political, social, and religious principles which are ultimately to permeate the nations.

CHAPTER III.

THE OVERTHROW IN THE WEST: GERMANIC INVASIONS.

In the interpretation of his vision of the beast, John is told of its rise, temporary removal, and reappearance: "The beast that thou sawest was, and is not; and is about to come up out of the abyss, and to go into perdition" (Rev. 17. 8). Here the Roman world-power, the imperial dominion, is in view. In verse 11 the final king himself is similarly described. The symbol of the beast is thus employed to describe first the dominion and then its imperial head. This symbolic association of locality and ruler is found elsewhere in Scripture, and is illustrated in this very chapter. The seven heads of the beast, for example, are interpreted in both ways: "The seven heads are seven mountains, ... and they are seven kings" (v. 9, R.V.) The distinction between verses 8 and 11 may be observed in this way: in the first part of the chapter, verses 1-8, the beast is viewed as a whole, indicating world-wide government; in verse 11 the scope of the symbol is limited, the beast is a person, and is identified with one of the seven heads, or kings, he is "himself also an eighth, and is of the seven." With this individual we shall be occupied later.

A striking illustration of the symbolic use of the word "beast" to denote both a kingdom and the ruler over it is to be found in Dan. 7, where the following statements are made: "These great beasts, which are four, are four kings" (v. 17), and "The fourth beast shall be the fourth kingdom" (v. 23).

The statement of verse 8 seems, then, undoubtedly to refer to the Empire; it did exist, it ceased to be, and it will reappear. The assertion that it "is not" must not be taken to mean that the beast had ceased to exist in John's time. The present tense is to be regarded as prophetic. The verb "to be" often has the force of continuance of existence. The whole statement implies a past existence, a discontinuance of that existence, a future reappearance. In the vision recorded in the thirteenth chapter, John saw one of the heads of the beast "as though it had been smitten unto death." If, as seems probable, this head is imperialism, then the overthrow of imperial Rome is likewise indicated in that passage.

In the light, then, of the words: "The beast that thou sawest was, and is not," we may now consider how the Roman Empire was overthrown.

Disintegration of the Western Half.

We have seen that, at the accession of the Emperor Valentinian I. in A.D. 364, the Empire was divided into two parts. The succeeding century witnessed the disintegration of the western half. The cause was primarily from within. Augustus, the first Emperor, had instituted a policy of settling colonies of "barbarians" from northern Europe within the frontiers of the Empire. Later Emperors adopted the policy more generally. The significance of this lies in the fact that by the barbarians who had already been thus established in the Empire, the attacks were commenced which resulted in the dismemberment of its western provinces.

Alaric and the Goths.

At the close of the fourth century hordes of Gothic tribes from north-eastern and eastern Germany set out, under Alaric their chief, in quest of new lands. Settlements of these very Goths had already been established south of the Danube by the Imperial Government as allies of the Romans. After an excursion into Italy, in which they were temporarily checked, they poured, in 406, into defenceless Gaul. From thence Alaric returned to invade Italy, and three times in three years besieged Rome (408-410), eventually sacking the city. After his death, in 410, the Goths retired from Italy, entered Gaul, and permanently occupied the southern part of that country and a large part of Spain, where they were known as =Visigoths= (i.e., Western Goths).

Other Germanic tribes also streamed into Gaul. Of these, the =Franks= (whence the name France) issued from districts around the middle and lower Rhine and occupied northern Gaul; the =Suevi=, from north and north-west Germany, passed through into Spain; the =Alani=, formerly from eastern Europe, settled in west France and Spain; the =Burgundians=, from eastern Germany, seized that part of Gaul which eventually was named after them, Burgundy. The =Vandals=, from northern and central Germany, after being defeated by the Franks, crossed into Spain under their leader Genseric, and from thence established themselves in the province of Africa, in 429. This occupation of Gaul and Spain was soon perforce recognised by the Emperor at Rome. At the death of the Emperor Honorius, in 423, Rome exercised little more than a nominal authority over the greater part of the west.

From Britain the Roman troops were withdrawn by Honorius, in 409, though the final abandonment of the island province did not take place till 436. Teutonic tribes from North Europe were soon engaged in invading this part of the Empire. The =Jutes=, from Jutland, landed in 449, the =Saxons= in 477, and about the same time the =Angles=.

Attila and the Huns.

Toward the close of the reign of Valentinian III. (433-455), Gaul and Italy were invaded by the =Huns= under Attila. The Huns originally inhabited a large part of central and northern Asia. In the latter part of the fourth century they moved west into Scythia and Germany, driving the Goths before them. Attila's dominions thereafter extended over a vast area of eastern, central, and northern Europe, and he was regarded as of equal standing with the Emperors at Constantinople and Rome. After a gigantic but futile incursion into Gaul, in 451, the Huns rushed into Italy, ravaging its northern plains. An embassy from Rome and an immense ransom saved the situation. Attila died in 453, and Italy was evacuated. The Huns eventually settled in south-eastern Europe, and their dominion dwindled away. A trace of their name may be found in the word Hungary.

Genseric and the Vandals.

In North Africa Genseric the Vandal established a powerful dominion, and set about preparing an invasion of Italy by sea. In 455 (the last year of the reign of Valentinian III.) his army of Vandals and Moors attacked Rome, which was again given over to pillage. Its wealth and treasures were transported to Carthage, and with them the vessels of the temple at Jerusalem; these had been brought to Rome in A.D. 70 by Titus, the conqueror of Jerusalem. For twenty years after Genseric's achievement Roman Emperors existed in little else than name, the real power being in the hands of a barbarian officer. In 476 the last Emperor was deposed by Odoacer, the king of the Heruli, a tribe which, issuing from the shores of the Baltic, made successful inroads into Italy and occupied much of the country. Odoacer was, at the request of the Roman Senate, given the reins of government by the eastern Emperor Zeno, and news was despatched to the court at Constantinople that no longer was there an Emperor of the west. Subsequently, in 493, Odoacer was slain by Theodoric, the king of the =Ostrogoths=, who then became predominant in the Italian peninsula. The Ostrogoths (i.e., Eastern Goths) had broken off from the main body of their nation, and after settling south of the Danube moved into the province of Dalmatia.

Northern Limits of the Empire.

Other Germanic tribes, in addition to those named above, firmly established themselves within the northern limits of the Empire. Of these, two are worthy of mention, the =Alemanni=, who occupied most of what is now Switzerland and districts northward, and the =Lombards=, who settled in north Italy and the territory north-east of it.

The Ten Kingdoms not Formed by the Germanic Invasions.

There have been various attempts to identify with the ten prophetic kingdoms the states formed from the western half of the Roman Empire by the Germanic tribes from the north. Such attempts fail from the standpoints both of history and of prophecy. To group the tribes so as to make ten kingdoms out of them is, of course, possible in several ways, for there were at least eighteen such tribes. Accordingly lists put forward differ considerably. But such grouping is manifestly arbitrary. Again, since these invading nations occupied only the western half of the Empire, the above allocation of the ten kingdoms necessarily leaves the eastern half out of consideration, and therefore excludes the land of Palestine from this stage of the prophetic forecast.

Now the prophecies concerning the times of the Gentiles are invariably focussed upon the Jews and their land. The dealings of God with the Jews form the pivot of His dealings with other nations. Thus no scheme of prophetic exposition relative to this subject is to be regarded as Scriptural which excludes Palestine from its scope. To endeavour to make the Word of God square with facts of history is to tamper with Scripture and to run the risk of obscuring its meaning and force.

The idea that the formation of the ten kingdoms took place in the fifth century fails to stand the test of Scripture in other respects. Of the ten kings prophecy foretells that "they receive authority as kings with the beast for one hour," that they "have one mind, and they give their power and authority unto the beast" (Rev. 17. 13, 14). No such tenfold confederacy has existed in Europe; it certainly never existed among the chieftains of the Germanic tribes which invaded the west of the Roman Empire in the fifth century, neither is there any record of such an agreement among them. Nor, again, can it be said that they made war with the Lamb and were overcome by Him (v. 14). These prophecies still await fulfilment. Similar considerations apply to the passage in Daniel 7 in reference to the fourth kingdom. The ten kings, it is said, would arise out of that kingdom, and after them another king who would make war with the saints and prevail against them until the Ancient of Days came (vv. 21, 22, 24).

Again, since the persecution under the king who arises after the others continues until the Ancient of Days comes (v. 22), his war against the saints must have lasted from the fifth century until the present time, if he arose in that century. Moreover, as he was said to be going to subdue three kingdoms (v. 24), the seven kingdoms not so subdued must likewise have continued. This has obviously not been the case. From every point of view it is impossible to assign the tenfold division to any time in the past.

CHAPTER IV.

THE OVERTHROW IN THE EAST: THE TURKISH EMPIRE.

Having narrated the disintegration of the western half of the Empire, we will now recount the events which involved the overthrow of the eastern half. The impoverishment of the imperial power at Rome, and the weakening effect of the Germanic attacks upon it, tended to enhance the power of the Emperor at Constantinople. Indeed the eastern Empire was soon regarded as the more important of the two, and for some time after the barbarian invasions in Italy the Emperors at Constantinople claimed supremacy over the west.

Mohammed and the Khaliphs.

The seventh century saw the ascendency of Mohammed (born A.D. 570) in Arabia, to which country his personal power, temporal and religious, was limited. Upon his death, in 632, his followers determined on the invasion of Persia and the Asiatic dominions of the Emperor at Constantinople. Mohammed's successor, Abubekr, the first of the Khaliphs (i.e., "representatives" of the prophet), at once waged war in both directions. Persia speedily succumbed; Syria and Palestine were subjugated after seven years by the Khaliph Omar. The reduction of Egypt followed, and during the remainder of this century the Saracens, the name by which the followers of Mohammed became termed in Christendom, extended their territory across the entire length of North Africa, and shortly afterwards even into Spain, where they overpowered the then disunited Visigoths.

The Saracen power in Western Asia was distracted during the next century by civil war, and was further weakened by unsuccessful wars against the Greeks. At length, in 750, the seat of government was moved from Damascus to Bagdad. From the eighth century onward, though the religion of Mohammed gained ground, and continues to do so to-day, the empire established by his followers dwindled rapidly, one province after another shaking off its allegiance until at the end of the tenth century its shattered dominions lay open to the nearest invader. The foe appeared in the shape of the formidable Turk.

Eastern Empire at End of 10th Century.

In view of the entrance of this new enemy we may note the extent of the territory belonging at this time to the eastern branch of the old Roman world, the Byzantine Empire, as it is termed (from Byzantium, the ancient name of Constantinople). The Eastern Emperors had recovered some of their lost ground in Asia, and at the close of the tenth century they held all Asia Minor, Armenia, a part of Syria, a considerable portion of Italy, and all the Balkan Peninsula.

The Appearance of the Turks.

Beyond the north-eastern border of the Saracen dominions lay the country of Turkestan, inhabited by the Turks, a branch of the warlike nation of the Tartars of Central Asia. With them the Saracens, after the establishment of their Government at Bagdad, waged successful warfare for a time, taking numbers of Turks captive and dispersing them over the Empire. This only facilitated the eventual downfall of the Saracen sovereignty. The Turks in Western Asia grew in influence, and at length the Turkish troops, breaking into open revolt, assumed control over the Khaliphate, deposing and nominating the Khaliphs at their will.

The Turks Embrace Mohammedanism.

Early in the eleventh century the bulk of the Turkish nation, under its leader Tongrol Bek, moving out from Turkestan, swept down upon Persia. The Khaliphate at Bagdad was, however, permitted to remain, and not only so, but Tongrol Bek and all his tribes embraced the Mohammedan religion. The invaders then marched west in vast numbers to make an attack upon Christendom, and in the course of time subdued Armenia and most of Asia Minor. Europe became alarmed, and the Byzantine Emperors eagerly sought the assistance of the nations of the west. Hence arose the Crusades, which had as their chief object the deliverance of Palestine from both Saracens and Turks, and which served to retard, though not to prevent, the advance of the Turkish power in Europe.

The Turks Enter Europe.

Early in the thirteenth century a mighty movement of Mongols south-west from Central Asia, involving the immediate destruction of the Khaliphate at Bagdad, exerted an important influence upon the Turks, in driving those Turkish tribes which had remained east of Armenia westward into Asia Minor. This resulted in the establishment of various Turkish dynasties in that country. At the close of the thirteenth century the paramount power over these was exercised by Osman (or Othman, whence the name Ottoman), who seized all that remained of the ancient Roman world in Asia, and thus practically founded the Ottoman Empire. In the middle of the fourteenth century the way was opened for the Ottomans to advance into Europe. They were invited by one of the rival factions at Constantinople to undertake their cause. The Turks accordingly crossed the Hellespont and seized Gallipoli and the territory in the vicinity of the capital. Constantinople itself was left unattacked for the time. Under Murad I., the grandson of Osman, Roumania and several kingdoms south of the Danube, including Bulgaria, were subdued. The kings of Hungary, Bosnia and Serbia rose against the invader, but were severely defeated, and by the decisive victory of Kosovo, in 1389, Serbia and Bosnia were annexed.

Constantinople Taken.

Constantinople was temporarily saved by another advance of the Mongol Tartars upon the Turkish dominions in Asia, where, in 1402, the Ottomans suffered a severe defeat. From this check they recovered, and during the first part of the fifteenth century were at war with the Hungarians and neighbouring races, whom they eventually overthrew. In 1451 Mohammed II. ascended the Ottoman throne, and in 1453 led an immense army against Constantinople. The city was taken by storm, the last of the Roman Emperors of the east died fighting, and Mohammed II. rode in triumph to the cathedral of St. Sophia, where he established the Moslem worship.

For over a hundred years after this the Turkish Empire continued to extend. Egypt was annexed in 1517, and in the middle of this century Tripoli and Algeria were added, as well as considerable districts in Europe and Asia. The Turks were now at the zenith of their power.

A Comparison of the Two Divisions.

Recapitulating, we may compare the two divisions of the Roman Empire since their overthrow, from the prophetic, religious and political standpoints. From the prophetic point of view our interest in the west has thus far centred in the fact that the ten kingdoms were not formed by the fifth century invasions; our interest in the east centres chiefly in the land of Palestine, wrenched, as we have seen, from the eastern Emperor by the Saracens, and then occupied by the Turks, who still possess it. From the religious standpoint, the Germanic tribes in the west accepted Roman Catholicism, hence its progress in that part of Europe; in the east the Turks had accepted Mohammedanism when invading the Empire of the Khaliphs, hence the establishment of Islamism throughout the Turkish dominions. Politically, the western invasion in the fifth century, and the consequent amalgamation of the Teutonic tribes with the peoples formerly under Roman control, led eventually to the formation of the various mediaeval monarchies of Western Europe which are to-day either kingdoms or republics. Affairs in the eastern half of the Roman world have moved more slowly in this respect, owing to the prolonged existence of the Ottoman Empire. The slow decay of the Turkish power from the middle of the sixteenth century onward has already resulted in the formation of some Eastern States, and the process still continues.

The Decline of the Turkish Empire.

The decline of the power of the Turks set in during the latter half of the sixteenth century, when their dominions passed under incapable rulers. In the reign of Selim II. (1566-1574) occurred the first conflict between the Turks and Russians, the former being driven back from Astrakkan. In 1593, during a war between Turkey and Austria, the provinces of Transylvania, Moldavia, and Wallachia rose in revolt. As the result of intermittent wars in the latter half of the seventeenth century Austria acquired almost the whole of Hungary. In 1770 Russia occupied Moldavia and Wallachia, which though nominally for a time under Turkey were practically Russian protectorates. During the next few years Russia regained the Crimea and all the neighbouring district north of the Black Sea. At the commencement of the nineteenth century the Ottoman Empire was in a perilous condition. Napoleon had plans for its partition. Provincial governors were everywhere acting independently of the Sultan. In 1804 Serbia revolted, and after a few years of persistent struggle obtained its autonomy. Greece revolted in 1820, and, though subdued for a time, gained its independence in 1829 through the intervention of England, France, and Russia, and chiefly as the result of the naval battle of Navarino, in which the Turco-Egyptian fleet was annihilated. In the same year Algeria was annexed by the French. European rivalries prevented for a time any rapid diminution of the Empire.

The Crimean War of 1854-5 had important consequences for the Balkan peoples. It gave them, under the slackening grasp of the Porte, twenty years of comparatively quiet national development. In 1860 Wallachia and Moldavia formed themselves into the single state of Roumania. In 1866 the Pasha of Egypt assumed the title of Khedive (i.e., king), thereby securing a measure of independence for the country. In 1875 the misrule of the Sultan led to the insurrection of Bosnia, Herzegovina, and Bulgaria. Serbia and Montenegro then took up arms. In 1877 a war with Russia saw Turkey without an ally. A complete Russian victory in 1878 issued in the treaties first of San Stefano and then of Berlin, by which Turkey yielded to Russia the state of Bessarabia and districts south of the Caucasus, the independence of Serbia, Montenegro, and Roumania were recognised by the Porte, Bulgaria was constituted an autonomous state, Bosnia and Herzegovina were ceded to Austria, Thessaly to Greece, and Cyprus to Britain. In 1885, as the result of a revolution, Eastern Roumelia became united to Bulgaria. Shortly after that date German influence began to gain ascendancy at the court of the Sultan, and, among other affairs, largely dominated the granting of railway concessions in Western Asia. The effects of that influence have been evidenced in the present war. In 1912 Italy annexed Tripoli after a brief war. In 1913 a short but sanguinary war with the Balkan States deprived Turkey of all her European dominions save for a small piece of territory in the vicinity of Constantinople. Egypt, which has been chiefly under British control for a considerable period, has in 1915 been practically annexed by Britain as a protectorate, the Khedive being deposed and a nominee of the British Government being placed in authority. Britain has likewise annexed a district north of the Persian Gulf.

The Coming Overthrow.

The continual decrease of the Turkish Empire, and more especially during the past hundred years, affords ground, apart from other considerations, for the expectation of its overthrow and the eventual cession of Palestine to the Jews, perhaps by a general agreement among the European Powers, events which seem not far distant. National jealousies would not permit the permanent annexation of Palestine by any one of these Powers, in whatever way the remaining Asiatic Turkish dominions may be divided. A proposal has already been put forward for its annexation to Egypt. Such an arrangement would in any case be merely temporary. To the Jews the land belongs, and by Divine decree the Jews are to possess it again.

[Illustration: The Turkish Empire in 1914.]

A Blank in Prophecy.

It should be observed, in passing, that Scripture is apparently silent concerning the occupation of Palestine by the Saracens and Turks. Such silence is noticeable when we remember how definitely the occupation by the other Gentile powers, the Chaldean, Medo-Persian, Greek, and Roman, and the order and character of their rule, were predicted. The cause of the silence is not difficult to ascertain. The four Gentile powers just mentioned had to do with the Jews as the recognised possessors of Palestine, either by way of removing them from their country or restoring them to it, or during such time as they were permitted to remain in it with liberty to continue their temple worship and sacrifice. The Chaldeans removed the Jews from the land, the Medo-Persians repatriated them, the Greeks permitted their continuance in it, the Romans did so too, until A.D. 70, when they crushed them. When, however, the Saracens and the Turks seized the land the Jews had been scattered, nor have they received national recognition while under them. Gentile occupation of Palestine during such times as the Jews remain in their present condition seems therefore to receive no direct notice in prophecy.

The restoration of Palestine to the Jews is closely connected with the revival of the Roman Empire in its tenfold form. Prior to considering the manner of this revival we must notice how during the period between the overthrow of that Empire and its coming resuscitation, its dominions and their government have remained Roman in character, thus affording a further proof that the coming and final world-power will not be entirely a new one, but will be a revival of the ancient Roman or fourth empire indicated in the prophecies of Daniel.

The Continuation of Roman Government and Influence.

Such was the prestige of the Roman name and authority that the chieftains of the Germanic tribes which in the fifth century subdued the western half of the Empire governed the conquered territories, not so much as tribal chiefs, but as successors to, and in continuation of, the imperial rule; they introduced no radical changes in the provincial and municipal forms of government of their predecessors. Civil organisation remained distinctly Roman, and has continued so; upon it are based some of the chief municipal institutions of modern life. Indeed Roman civil law still remains the foundation of modern jurisprudence.

In south-eastern Europe, too, countries which were for centuries under the power of the Turk retained, in their municipal institutions and organisation, the impress of Roman authority. It should be remembered that though the eastern or Byzantine portion of the ancient Roman Empire was distinct from the western, its emperors being designated as Grecian in contrast to the Roman, yet its legislative foundations were laid in the Roman Empire prior to the division of the east from the west. Byzantine imperialism was therefore really Roman under an eastern title. According as the states in the east have become freed from the Turkish yoke, so the character of their government and legislation has conformed in a large degree to those of the west. The further diminution of the Turkish Empire will doubtless see a corresponding revival of western conditions and methods.

Roman Imperialism Continued.

It is important also to observe that notwithstanding the passing away of the Roman Empire as such, the principle of imperialism remained, and, amidst the vicissitudes of national government in Europe, has continued to the present time. The imperial power in the west was not abolished when in 476 the last Roman Emperor was deposed. On the contrary, there was a kind of reunion imperially of the west with the east. For a considerable time the tribal kings of the west received recognition from the eastern emperors, and were regarded as their associates in imperial control. This was the case even with the Saxon kings in Britain, and on Saxon coins may be seen to-day the same title, basileus (i.e., king), as was borne by the emperors at Constantinople. Italy itself was wrested from the Teutons by the eastern Emperor Justinian in the sixth century, and remained under the Byzantine Caesars till 731.

Meanwhile the Roman Senate continued to exercise its authority, and in 800 chose the Frankish king Charlemagne as their sovereign. He was already ruling over the greater part of Western Europe, and was now crowned as Emperor at Rome by the Pope. Though his empire fell to pieces after his death, his dominions retained, and have since retained, their Roman character.

Consideration of space forbids our tracing here the further continuance of imperialism as a factor in European politics. Recent history and present-day events indicate how rapidly we are approaching its final development at the close of the times of the Gentiles. The coming confederacy of European states will not result in the formation of a new empire, but will be the revival of the Roman in an altered form.

CHAPTER V.

THE COMING REVIVAL OF THE ROMAN EMPIRE.

(1) The Geographical Standpoint.

The coming revival of the Roman Empire will for our present purpose be best considered from the geographical, political, and religious standpoints.

Geographical Considerations.

Any forecast of the exact delimitations of the ten kingdoms constituting the reconstructed Empire must necessarily be largely conjectural. That their aggregate area will precisely conform to that of the ancient Roman Empire does not necessarily follow from the fact of its revival, and cannot be definitely concluded from Scripture. An extension of the territories of the Empire in its resuscitated form would be quite consistent with the retention of its identity. Moreover, if Roman imperialism may be considered to have continued in the hands of Teutonic monarchs after the fall of the western part of the Empire in 476, if, for instance, Charles the Great, of whom we have spoken (p. 58), ruled as a Roman Emperor, despite the passing away of the actual Empire itself, then the dominions which were under the rule of these later monarchs may yet be found incorporated in the Empire, and so form parts of the ten kingdoms. In that case Germany and Holland would be included. Possibly, too, the Empire will embrace all the territories which belonged to the three which preceded it, the Grecian, Medo-Persian, and Chaldean. Certainly when the stone fell on the toes of the image, the whole image, representing these former three as well as the fourth, was demolished. Suggestive also in this respect is the fact that the beast in the vision recorded in Revelation 13. 2 was possessed of features of the leopard, the bear, and the lion, the same beasts which represented in Daniel's vision the Grecian, Medo-Persian, and Chaldean kingdoms (Dan. 7. 4-6), the order in Revelation 13 being inverted. While political characteristics are doubtless chiefly in view in these symbols, there may at the same time be an indication of the eventual incorporation of the first three empires in the fourth. It must be remembered, too, that the authority of the federal head of the ten kingdoms is to be world-wide: "There was given to him authority over every tribe and people and tongue and nation" (Rev. 13. 7). It is probable, therefore, that while the ten kingdoms will occupy a well defined area, their dependencies and the countries which are allied with them will embrace practically the remainder of the world.

If, on the other hand, the Roman Empire is to be reconstructed in exact conformity territorially with its ancient boundaries--such a reconstruction is, of course, not inconceivable--we must consider what period of the conquests of the ancient Empire to take, whether under the first emperor, Augustus, or during the Apostolic Age, or later. We may, perhaps, be helped by the facts already mentioned, that prophecy relating to Gentile dominion is focussed upon the Jews and Palestine, and has especially in view the presence of the nation in their land. Now, shortly after their overthrow, in A.D. 70, their national recognition as possessors of the land ceased. This period, moreover, corresponds broadly to the close of the Apostolic Age. The dispersion of the Jews among the nations was completed by Adrian in the next century. He desolated the whole of Palestine, expelling all the remaining Jewish inhabitants.

A Review of the Ancient Territories.

We will therefore now review the limits of the Empire and of some of its provinces at that time, noticing certain circumstances of past and present history suggestive of future issues. In doing so we are not predicting that the boundaries of the revived Empire will be those of the ancient.

Commencing with North Africa, it will be observed, on referring to the map, that practically the same strip of territory which belonged to the Roman Empire in the times of the apostles has passed directly under the government of countries which were themselves then within the Empire. For Spain rules over Morocco, France over Algeria and Tunis, Italy recently seized Tripoli, and Britain has, since Turkey's entrance into the great war, virtually taken possession of Egypt. It seems not a little significant that no country which was outside the limits of the Empire at the time under consideration has been permitted by God to annex these North African territories since the Saracens and the Turks were dispossessed of them.

Passing now to Asia, the territory in that continent which belonged to Rome in the first century is approximately what remained to Turkey immediately prior to the present war. Mesopotamia and most of Armenia were included. The war has already seen Turkey dispossessed of portions of these. The downfall of the Turkish Empire would almost certainly involve territorial rearrangements of deepest import in the light of prophecy, especially as regards Palestine.

Divisions of the Greek Empire: A Possible Renewal.

The 8th chapter of Daniel apparently indicates that the Asiatic territories of the Empire will be divided much as they were under the Greeks after the death of Alexander the Great. He was obviously symbolised by the great horn (v. 22). The four horns which came up in its place (v. 8) are clearly, too, the four generals who succeeded Alexander, and among whom his dominions were divided, Cassander ruling over Macedonia and Greece, Lysimachus over part of Asia Minor and Thrace (the extent of the latter province was almost exactly what now belongs to Turkey in Europe), Seleucus over most of Syria, Palestine, Mesopotamia, and the east, and Ptolemy over Egypt. Next follows a prediction carrying us to events which are evidently yet future. It is said, for instance, that these events will take place "in the latter time of their kingdom (not, it will be observed, in the time of the four kings themselves who succeeded Alexander, but of the kingdoms over which they ruled), when the transgressors are come to the full" (v. 23). The expressions in this chapter, "the time of the end" (v. 17), "the latter time of the indignation," "the appointed time of the end" (v. 19), and "the latter time of their kingdom" (v. 23), all point to a period still future, namely, to the close of the present age. Again, in reference to the "king of fierce countenance," while much of the prophecy can be applied to Antiochus Epiphanes in the second century B.C., yet no man has hitherto arisen whose character and acts have been precisely those related in verses 9-12 and 23-25. We may also compare what is said of "the transgression that maketh desolate" (v. 13) with the Lord's prophecy concerning the abomination of desolation (Matt. 24. 15-22), a prophecy which also manifestly awaits fulfilment.

Possibly, therefore, these Asiatic territories will be similarly divided in the coming time. In regard to the first of the above-mentioned four divisions, the recent extension of Greece to include the ancient province of Macedonia is remarkable. This was an outcome of the Balkan War of 1912. The boundaries of Greece are now approximately what they were under Cassander in the time of the Grecian Empire, what they were also later as the provinces of Macedonia and Achaia in the Roman Empire. There has lately, therefore, been a significant reversion to ancient conditions in this respect.

Other European Territories.

Coming now to the dual-monarchy of Austria-Hungary, reference to the map of the Roman Empire in the Apostolic Age will show that what are now Hungary, Transylvania, Bessarabia, and other states of the present monarchy were without the Roman boundaries, while Pannonia, or what is now Austria west of the Danube, was within; even when in the next century Dacia (now

Transylvania, Bessarabia, &c.) was annexed, the two parts of the present dual kingdom were separate. The separation of Hungary from Austria has for a considerable time been a practical question of European politics, and may be hastened by present events.

The northern and north-eastern boundaries of Italy embraced the Trentino and the peninsula of Istria. Noticeable, therefore, are the present efforts of Italy to acquire these very districts, efforts which seem likely to achieve success. Roman states north of Italy covered what are now Baden, Wurtemberg, Luxemberg, and a large part of Bavaria. The possibility of an eventual severance of these from Prussian domination has been much discussed of late.

The Rhenish provinces of Alsace and Lorraine, originally portions of the Roman province of Gallia (now France), were snatched from France by Germany in the Franco-Prussian war of 1870-71. Their recovery is a supreme object of the efforts of the French in the present war, and not without hope of success.

The British Empire.

As to Britain, at the time under consideration the greater part of the island was definitely included in the Roman Empire. Ireland and most of Scotland were never conquered by the Romans. Should Britain form one of the ten kingdoms, there is nothing to show that Ireland or any other part of the British Empire must of necessity be absolutely separated from it. Self-government may yet be possessed by those territories which have not yet received it, and it is significant that Ireland has now practically obtained it. That the lands which are linked with Britain as dependencies, or as in possession of self-government, should remain as integral parts of the Empire is but consistent with the coming world-wide authority of the potentate who will be the federal head of the ten kingdoms. And that each state in the British Empire should have its own local government is, on the other hand, consistent with the establishment of a closer and complete confederacy of ten kingdoms, the area of which may correspond largely to that of the ancient Roman Empire. In contrast to the self-government of the other countries of the world at the coming period, the ten united kingdoms will eventually be absolutely under the control of the final emperor just mentioned, for the ten kings over these states, who receive authority as kings with him, will be of one mind to give their power and authority and their kingdom to him (Rev. 17. 12, 13, 17).

What has been said of the British Empire may be true also of others of the ten kingdoms which have colonies or dependencies, and thus, while the ten kingdoms will themselves constitute an Empire, their alliances and treaties with other countries of the world will apparently involve an extension of the authority of the controlling despot "over every tribe and people and tongue and nation" (Rev. 13. 7). If, for instance, the United States of America were at that time in alliance with Britain (quite a possible contingency), their joint influence would probably extend to the whole of the American continents, which would thereby acknowledge his authority.

We may observe, too, the way in which the continent of Africa has come under certain European influences in modern times. The mention of this is simply suggestive. That the Scripture will be absolutely fulfilled is beyond doubt; the exact mode of its accomplishment is known to God.

(2) The Political Standpoint.

European Federation.

Agencies are already at work for the establishment of a confederacy of European States--not the least significant of the many signs that the end of the age is approaching. The movement towards confederacy is doubtless receiving an impetus from the great upheaval in Europe. A circular issued in December, 1914, and distributed far and wide, announced the formation of a committee of influential men with the object of promoting a "European Federation." The circular says: "In sight of the present situation of ruin it ought to be the general opinion that a firmer economical and political tie is of utmost importance for all nations without exception, and that particularly for Europe the narrower bond of a federation, based on equality and interior independence of all partaking states, is of urgent necessity, which public opinion ought to demand."

A pamphlet published by the Committee recommends that the union of states shall be economical, political, and legal, with an international army as a common guarantee, and that European Federation should become the principal and most urgent political battle-cry for the masses of all European nations, and declares that "when the Governments are willing, when the public opinion of all peoples forces them to be willing, there is no doubt but that a reasonable and practical union of nations will prove to be as possible and natural as is at present a union of provinces, cantons, territories, whose populations often show more difference of race and character than those of nations now at hostilities." The Committee calls upon the peoples of Europe to suffer the diplomatists no longer to dispose of them like slaves and by militarism to lash them to fury against each other. It calls upon them to see to it that never and nowhere should a member of any body or Government be elected who is not an advocate of the Federation, and that the trade union, society, or club to which any individual belongs should express sympathy with the movement in meetings and in votes. "The people," it is said, "have it now in their power, more than ever before, to control the Powers."

Two Possible Ways of Federation.

The formation of ten federated states, covering at least the area of the ancient Empire at the end of the first century of the present era, may be effected in two ways, either by the peaceful methods of arbitration and treaty, or as a result of strife and confusion. That the present European War will be succeeded by efforts for the creation of permanent international harmony and universal peace is probable, as is also some attempt at such a federation as is proposed by the above-mentioned Committee. On the other hand, sinister indications abound to-day which point to industrial strife and revolution rather than peace. The condition of the industrial world presents a gloomy prospect indeed. There are ominous signs of keener conflict than ever between capital and labour. The forces of Socialism, Syndicalism, Communism, &c., are rapidly increasing in power and in international activity, and their avowed aims presage anything but peace in the near future. We may take, for example, the declared objects of "The Alliance of the Social Democracy"--now incorporated in the International Working Men's Association--"To destroy all States and all Churches with all their institutions and laws, religious, political, juridical, financial, magisterial, academical, economical, and social, and to establish in their place industrial co-operation and collective ownership of land and capital." All this sounds very pretentious, and would probably fail of complete accomplishment, but the agencies at work for it are strong. Attempts on a large scale would certainly lead to unprecedented disorder and chaos.

The Sea Symbolic of National Unrest.

Not improbably the ten kingdoms of the reconstructed Roman Empire will arise as a result of political and social confusion. Thus it was in the case of the French Revolution and the consequent uprising of Napoleon. A repetition of such events on a far wider scale in the future is quite conceivable. In the prophetic vision given to the Apostle John, the beast was seen "coming up out of the sea" (Rev. 13. 1). Now the sea is in Scripture used figuratively of the nations, its characteristic restlessness symbolising their commotion and strife. Compare the words of Isaiah: "Ah, the uproar of many peoples, which roar like the roaring of the seas; and the rushing of nations, that rush like the rushing of many waters! The nations shall rush like the rushing of many waters: but He shall rebuke them" (Isa. 17. 12, 13; see also Psa. 65. 7; and Ezek. 26. 3). To national unrest the Lord Jesus applied similar language when He foretold to the disciples that there would be "upon the earth distress of nations, in perplexity for the roaring of the sea and the billows; men fainting for fear, and for expectation of the things which are coming on the world" (Luke 21. 25, 26). So also the waters which John had seen in his vision are described by the angel as "peoples, and multitudes, and nations, and tongues" (Rev. 17. 15). Daniel, too, saw the four great beasts come up from the sea as a result of the breaking forth of the four winds of the Heaven upon it, an undoubted representation of a condition of national disturbance (Dan. 7. 2, 3).

That the beast of Revelation 13. 1 was seen coming up out of the sea points, therefore, to the probability that the ten kings who will have brief authority over the revived Empire will be raised to their kingdom, not by constitutional methods, but as the result of revolutions and the collapse of present-day governments and institutions.

Revolutions and their Issues.

Should any great measure of success attend the syndicalist and communist movements of the day, and especially if they are internationalised, the inevitable revolutions and disorder would almost certainly issue, as revolutions have so frequently issued, in despotism and autocracy, and perhaps in this way the ten kings would arise. The overthrow of the governments in the countries involved would remove what has certainly been the great restraint upon lawlessness[A] from the times of the apostles until now. Everything would be ripe for the appearance of a universal potentate. The cry would arise for "a man," a controlling organiser to bring order out of chaos. The unstable character of the rule of the ten kings, and the impoverishment of their kingdoms, would lead them, as a matter of diplomacy, to hand over their authority to him.

[A] See "The Epistles to the Thessalonians, with Notes Exegetical and Expository," by C. F. Hogg and W. E. Vine, note c. pp. 259, 260. (Glasgow: Pickering & Inglis. 3/9, p.f.)

The Iron and the Clay.

The political constitution of the successive empires during "the time of the Gentiles" was indicated in the image of Nebuchadnezzar's vision by the various substances of which the parts of the image were composed. While the regular deterioration in the relative value of these substances is noticeable, we are concerned now with those of the legs and feet. The legs were of iron, and the feet part of iron and part of potter's clay, not moist or miry clay, but "earthenware" (Dan. 2. 41, R.V., margin), and consequently brittle (v. 42, margin).

That the iron symbolised militarism seems clear from what is said of the fourth kingdom, that "as iron breaketh in pieces and subdueth all things: and as iron that crusheth all these, shall it break in pieces and crush" (v. 40). Nations are broken and crushed by military power, and thus the nations were treated by the Romans. This was further signified by the iron teeth of the fourth beast, as is definitely stated in Daniel 7. 19, 23: "And shall devour the whole earth, and shall tread it down, and break it in pieces."

The supposition that the clay represents democracy is gratuitous and arbitrary. The early Roman Empire, symbolised by the legs of the image, was built up under democratic rule. When republicanism was superseded by imperialism, democratic principles still prevailed. Democracy, therefore, played its part from the very commencement of the fourth kingdom, and had it been symbolised by the clay, not only the feet and toes but the legs themselves would have consisted of mingled iron and clay. Moreover, democracy in the generally accepted sense of the term has not always been found to be of an unstable or brittle character; witness the republicanism of the United States. Democracies, too, may be established on strictly constitutional principles.

Another explanation, therefore, of the symbolism of the clay must be sought, and it is not unlikely to be found in those revolutionary principles to which we have already referred, which were evidenced at the time of the French Revolution, and are finding expression, though in greater variety to-day, in such projects as those of the International Working Men's Association. Certainly the masses of the people of Europe are being permeated both by militarism and by the revolutionary doctrines of which we have spoken. Should these principles spread among the civil services and forces, everything would be in a complete state of preparedness for Unprecedented Political and Social Upheaval

which would effect the overthrow of present forms of government. From the world's point of view the situation would require a consummate genius with powers of world-wide organisation. Doubtless Satan's masterpiece of infidel ingenuity would be at hand for the occasion.

We are not predicting that this is to be the manner of the revival of the Empire and of the advent of its imperial head. We have merely suggested possible circumstances in the light of Scripture and present-day movements. The actual circumstances attending the rise of the ten kings and their Emperor must for the time remain conjectural. Certainly these kings will receive authority with him for one hour (Rev. 17. 12), a phrase which may be translated "at the same time;" and certainly they will agree to give their power and authority to him (v. 13).

(3) The Religious Standpoint.

We will now note the religious conditions which are to prevail for a time upon the resuscitation of the Empire. These are plainly indicated for us in Revelation 17. The apostle sees a woman sitting on the seven-headed and ten-horned beast. The woman is gorgeously arrayed, holds in her hand a golden cup full of abominations, and is drunken with the blood of the saints. Her name, written on her forehead, is

"Mystery, Babylon the Great,"

"the mother of the harlots and of the abominations of the earth" (vv. 3-6). The woman is symbolically described as the city of Rome (v. 18), and that leads on to a second mention of Babylon, in chapter 18, and a new description. Now to the description of the woman in chapter 17 nothing more closely corresponds than the Papacy. But if the Babylon of chapter 17 is to be identified with that of chapter 18, the Papacy answers to the whole description only to a limited extent. While, however, there is much in common in the two descriptions in these chapters, yet the two Babylons are possibly to be distinguished. The Babylon of chapter 17 is a "mystery," not so that of chapter 18. Again, the destruction of the one is different from that of the other. The first will be destroyed by the ten kings and their emperor (17. 16), the second by the direct judgment of God (18. 5, 8, 20); the first as the result of human antagonism, the second by famine, fire and earthquake. We are perhaps, therefore, justified in taking the more limited view in connection with the circumstances of chapter 17. Even so the woman may be regarded as representing the apostate sacerdotal systems which have sprung from the Papacy as well as that system itself.

The position of the woman indicates an exercise of power which is voluntarily supported by the beast. That she sits upon the waters implies her religious dominion over the nations; that she is carried by the beast, who rules over the nations politically, implies that there will be a complete alliance between her and the ten kings with their chief, and that the sphere of her influence will be co-extensive with the dominions of the beast.

The Papacy: Its Present Power.

Now though the Papacy lost its temporal power in 1870, it is far from having lost its political influence. Ecclesiastically, too, though it has received various set-backs, it is manifestly gaining power. This is especially observable, for example, in Britain, the overthrow of which as a Protestant Power is undoubtedly the object of the persistent aggressiveness of Romanism. This aggressiveness is manifest in all the dominions of the British Empire, as well as in other lands.

Again, while certain governments have of late shaken off the ecclesiastical yoke, and infidelity has spread among the people of Roman Catholic lands, the number of Roman Catholics has increased with great rapidity. They were estimated at somewhat over 200,000,000 twenty years ago, they are now said to number about 300,000,000.

Indications are not wanting of a tendency towards

A Reunion of Christendom,

which would be facilitated by a willingness on the part of the Papacy to adapt itself to the impulse of the time.

Present events, therefore, point to a great renewal of Papal power involving the fulfilment of the prophecy relating to the woman and the beast that carries her. This renewed alliance between the political and the ecclesiastical powers will, however, be of brief duration. The successful efforts of governments in recent times to liberate themselves from Papal authority, as in the case of France and Portugal, are but foreshadowings of the eventual entire destruction of ecclesiasticism and sacerdotalism under the revived Roman Empire. "The ten horns ... and the beast, these shall hate the harlot, and shall make her desolate and naked, and shall eat her flesh, and shall burn her utterly with fire" (Rev. 17. 16). Thus it would seem that, when at the very zenith of its power and ambition, the Papacy, at the head of amalgamated Christendom, will suddenly meet its doom.

The Doom of Religious Babylon.

Its accumulated wealth would probably be an incentive in determining the ten kings to take this step, owing possibly to the impoverishment of their kingdoms as a result of wars and political and social upheavals. An additional cause will doubtless be the widespread spirit of antagonism against all religion.

Submission to the Papal yoke has invariably had an aftermath of infidelity; similarly the temporary subservience of the beast to the woman will issue in the casting off of all religious restraint and in the universal acknowledgment of the presumptuous claims of the world-ruler.

Satanic Authority of the Emperor.

The authority of this final emperor of the Roman kingdom will be Satanic. "The dragon gave him his power, and his throne, and great authority" (Rev. 13. 2); "the beast ... was, and is not; and is about to come up out of the abyss, and to go into perdition" (Rev. 17. 8). This implies that he has been on the earth in the past. The same thing is indicated in the interpretation of the seven heads. Topographically they are described as seven mountains, personally as seven kings (v. 9). Of these, five had fallen, the sixth was in power in John's time, the seventh had not then come (v. 10). The beast (clearly here symbolising, not a kingdom, but a person) would be an eighth, and yet would be of the seven (v. 11). These heads have been regarded by some as forms of government, by others as empires, or again, as emperors. There seems to be no reason why they are not to be regarded as emperors, though doubtless their empires are in view, as being associated with them. Accordingly, the fact that the eighth is also one of the seven indicates his reappearance on the scene. Various suggestions have been made as to his identification, but this must remain uncertain until his advent. With him the ten kings for a time receive authority (v. 12), subsequently handing it over to him with their kingdom (v. 17), but not before they have together with him crushed the great religious system symbolised by the woman (v. 16). His stupendous power and brilliant abilities, the evidence of his superhuman origin, his phenomenal capacity for organisation, and the consolidation of the empire under his absolute control will cause the whole world to marvel at him (Rev. 13. 3; 17. 8). To the world, in its divinely inflicted and therefore retributive delusion, he will appear like a god who has come to deliver from woe, and to introduce the long-looked-for age of peace and prosperity. Wonder will be succeeded by worship, both of the man and of Satan. "They worshipped the dragon, because he gave his authority unto the beast; and they worshipped the beast, saying, Who is like unto the beast? and who is able to war with him?" (13. 4).

The world is now in course of rapid preparation for all this:

The "Superman"

has of late become a much discussed topic in various classes of society and in the press, and the idea is supported by the theories of evolution which are receiving increasingly wide acceptance. A spirit of expectancy is being thus aroused which will undoubtedly facilitate the recognition of the man himself at his advent, and the acknowledgment of his claims to divine honour. But this will involve the worship of Satan, and to this end the effective agency of

Spiritism

has been long at work. Spiritism leads to devil worship. It must do so; its energising power is Satan himself. Both spiritism and theosophy, and similar forms of error, all of which are rapidly on the increase to-day, are paving the way for world-wide worship of the dragon.

The imperial power and worship of this emperor will be promoted by another potentate similarly energised by Satan. This latter is the second beast, described in Revelation 13. 11-end. Later on in the book he is called

The False Prophet

(Rev. 16. 13; 19. 20; 20. 10), indicating that his activities are chiefly of a religious character, and perhaps that he will be more closely connected with Jewish affairs. He will make "the earth and them that dwell therein worship the beast," the emperor of the ten kingdoms (13. 11), deceiving the world by supernatural signs wrought in the presence of the first beast (v. 12), and enforcing the worship of his image (v. 15), the abomination of desolation set up in the temple at Jerusalem (Matt. 24. 15). With the worship of an image the times of the Gentiles began (Dan. 3. 1), and with similar idolatry they will end. In the days of the early Roman emperors their deification was celebrated by the adoration of their images. Then, as formerly under Nebuchadnezzar, those who refused to worship suffered death. So will it be under the final emperor and his colleague.

Various opinions are held regarding these two beasts of Revelation 13, as to which is the Man of Sin spoken of by Paul in 2 Thessalonians 2, which the Antichrist mentioned in John's Epistles, and which of the two is the wilful king described in Daniel 11. Limitations of space preclude our entering into the subject in detail here. The present writer holds the view that all three are the same person, and that they are also the same as the horn in Daniel 7. 8, 11, and as the first beast of Revelation 13, and that these are all different descriptions of the final head of the revived Empire. The Old Testament passages somewhat briefly announce the arising of this world-wide ruler; the New Testament passages unfold and expand the preceding predictions concerning him, among the additional details given in the New Testament being the fact that he is to have a prophet who will assiduously support his claim to deity and his administration. It is the world-emperor, and not his prophet, who is to be worshipped, and who therefore proclaims himself as God (2 Thess. 2. 4). His prophet, the second beast of Revelation 13, in the exercise of all the power of the first, will cause the world to worship him (13. 12). As his prophet and prime minister he would not himself endeavour to usurp the position of him whose avowed deity he seeks to support.

The similarity of the details in the above-mentioned passages indicates that the same person is in view in each case. His blasphemies, for instance, and his assumption of deity are mentioned in Daniel 7. 25; 11. 36, 37; 2 Thessalonians 2. 3, 4, and Revelation 13. 5, 6, and his war with the saints in Daniel 7. 21, 25 and Revelation 13. 7. Further, the blasphemous proclamation of himself as God is consistent with what is said in John's Epistles concerning the Antichrist. For in his self-deification he is directly "antagonistic to Christ," he denies that Jesus is the Christ, and therefore denies the Father and the Son (1 John 2. 22).

The two potentates will establish not only a universal religion, but also a

Universal System of Commerce.

The second beast "causeth all, the small and the great, and the rich and the poor, and the free and the bond, that there be given them a mark on their hand, or upon their forehead; and that no man should be able to buy or to sell, save he that hath the mark, even the name of the beast or the number of his name" (Rev. 13. 16, 17). This indicates a world-wide protectionist system, such a system as, for instance, might conceivably be established under some form of syndicalism. Undeniably, circumstances in the industrial world to-day manifest an increasing tendency in this direction. The principles previously mentioned, as now making for industrial and international revolution, and the present stupendous movements towards amalgamation, are clearly preparing for the fulfilment of this prophecy by facilitating the eventual establishment of the unrighteous commercial system of the reconstituted Empire.

CHAPTER VI.

THE EVERLASTING KINGDOM.

We have now to consider the dealings of the two beasts, the final Roman emperor and his false prophet, with

The Jews.

With the Romans the Jews joined in the death of Christ, and with the rulers of this fourth empire they will be in agreement for a time at the close of their long course of apostasy. This was especially made known to Daniel in the prophecy of

The Seventy Weeks

(Dan. 9). These weeks (lit., hebdomads, or periods of seven, i.e., seven years each) had been divinely decreed (or "cut off," i.e., from the period of "the times of the Gentiles") upon his people and his city. From the going forth of the commandment to restore and to build Jerusalem unto the Anointed One (the Messiah), the Prince, would be seven weeks and threescore and two weeks. After this the Anointed One would be cut off, and would have nothing (Dan. 9. 24-26). This period is 69 times 7, or 483 years, and to the very day this was the period commencing with the command of Artaxerxes Longimanus, King of Persia, for the restoration of Jerusalem (Neh. 2. 1-9), and ending with the triumphal entry of Christ into the city (Matt. 21. 1-11).[B] Four days later He was crucified, "the Anointed One was cut off and had nothing," i.e., He did not enter then upon His Messianic kingdom. The prophecy predicted that the people of the prince (lit., "a prince") that would come would destroy the city and the sanctuary. That took place in A.D. 70, under Titus Vespasianus. But Titus is not "the prince that shall come." This, apart from other considerations, is clear from what follows: "And his (the prince's) end shall be with a flood (or rather, 'in the overflowing,' i.e., of the wrath of God)," a prediction at once inapplicable to Titus. The mention of

The Last "Week"

is deferred, indicating an interval between the sixty-ninth and the seventieth. Now the events predicted for the seventieth had no historical fulfilment immediately after the sixty-ninth. The one, therefore, did not follow the other consecutively. At the commencement of the intervening period the Jews were scattered from their land. At the seventieth they will have been restored, and the events of that week concern "the prince that shall come," the last world-emperor, and his dealings with them. "He shall make a firm covenant with many (lit., 'the many,' i.e., the great majority of the nation) for one week" (v. 27). This covenant is described in Isaiah's prophecies as a "covenant with death" and an "agreement with Hell." The covenant, he says, "shall be disannulled," and the agreement "shall not stand; when the overflowing scourge shall pass through, then ye shall be trodden down by it" (Isa. 28. 18). That this refers to a time yet future and not to past Israelitic history may be gathered from verse 22, where the theme and the language are similar to those of the passage in Daniel now under consideration. Daniel tells us the mode of the disannulling. "In the midst of the week (R.V., margin) he shall cause the sacrifice and oblation to cease." Accordingly after three and a half years the Antichrist, manifesting his real character, will prove himself a traitor and break the covenant, and thus Isaiah's prediction will be fulfilled.

[B] See "The Coming Prince," by Sir Robert Anderson. Price, 5/.

Apparently at the very time when he thus breaks his league with the Jews the Antichrist will determine upon his public deification and the establishment of his worship in the Temple. For he it is who "opposeth and exalteth himself above all that is called God, or that is worshipped; so that he as God sitteth in the Temple of God, showing himself that he is God" (2 Thess. 2. 4). This, with the setting up of his image, will doubtless be the fulfilment of the prophecies recorded by Daniel, that "upon the wing (or pinnacle) of abominations shall come one that maketh desolate" (Dan. 9. 27, cp. 11. 31 and 12. 11), and "they shall profane the sanctuary, even the fortress, and shall take away the continual burnt offering, and they shall set up the abomination that maketh desolate" (11. 31, cp. 12. 11); a fulfilment also of the Lord's prediction that "the abomination of desolation, which was spoken of by Daniel the prophet," will "stand in the holy place" (Matt. 24. 15). In the establishment of this blasphemous worship of the emperor, the false prophet will play a prominent part, as we have seen from the latter part of Revelation 13.

The many references to the desolator and the desolations are indicative of the

Fierce Persecution

which will follow. This will be at first directed against "the remnant," the large numbers of Jews who will repudiate allegiance to the beast and to the false prophet, many doubtless having been converted to their coming Messiah through the testimony of two witnesses who will be sent from God to the nation. "They shall prophesy a thousand two hundred and threescore days, clothed in sackcloth" (Rev. 11. 3-13). The success of their ministry will apparently arouse the bitter antagonism of Satan and his human instruments. The breaking of the covenant with the people as a whole indicates that an effort will also be made to crush the entire nation. Thus the latter half of the seventieth week will be the time of "Jacob's trouble," "a time of trouble, such as never was since there was a nation even to that same time" (Dan. 12. 1), though the unprecedented tribulation will not be confined to the Jews only.

Armageddon and After.

The bitter antagonism of the man of sin, and his colleague, the false prophet, against God and His people will culminate in the gathering together of all the forces of the Empire in Palestine in final conflict for the complete domination of the world. This tremendous event is thus indicated by the apostle John: "And I saw coming out of the mouth of the dragon, and out of the mouth of the beast, and out of the mouth of the false prophet, three unclean spirits, as it were frogs: for they are the spirits of devils (correctly, "demons"), working signs; which go forth unto the kings of the whole world, to gather them together unto the war of the great day of God, the Almighty" (Rev. 16. 13, 14).

In reality the issue at stake will be the supremacy of Christ or of Satan in the earth. The objective will be neither territorial conquest nor naval supremacy, nor commercial predominance. The war of the beast and the ten kings under him is against the Lamb (Rev. 17. 14). This the second Psalm had foretold: "Why do the nations rage, and the peoples imagine a vain thing? The kings of the earth set themselves, and the rulers take counsel together against the Lord, and against His Anointed, saying, Let us break their bands asunder, and cast away their cords from us." The issue is not uncertain: "He that sitteth in the Heavens shall laugh: the Lord shall have them in derision."

The Scene of the Conflict

is Har-Magedon, commonly known as Armageddon (Rev. 16. 16). The name, which is associated with Megiddo, a locality famed in Old Testament history for its decisive battles (Judges 5. 19; 2 Kings 23), doubtless stands here for a wider area, stretching, as we shall see, from the north to the south of the land.

The combatants, the conflict and its conclusion, are described by John in vivid language of terrible grandeur in Revelation 19. 11-21: "And I saw the Heaven opened; and behold, a white horse, and He that sat thereon, called Faithful and True; and in righteousness He doth judge and make war. And His eyes are a flame of fire, and upon his head are many diadems; and He hath a name written, which no one knoweth but He Himself. And He is arrayed in a garment sprinkled with blood: and His name is called the Word of God. And the armies which are in Heaven followed Him upon white horses, clothed in fine linen, white and pure. And out of His mouth proceedeth a sharp sword, that with it He should smite the nations: and He shall rule them with a rod of iron: and He treadeth the winepress of the fierceness of the wrath of Almighty God. And He hath on His garment and on His thigh a name written, KING OF KINGS, AND LORD OF LORDS.

"And I saw an angel standing in the sun; and he cried with a loud voice, saying to all the birds that fly in mid heaven, Come and be gathered together unto the great supper of God; that ye may eat the flesh of kings, and the flesh of captains, and the flesh of mighty men, and the flesh of horses and of them that sit thereon, and the flesh of all men, both free and bond, and small and great.

"And I saw the beast, and the kings of the earth, and their armies, gathered together to make war against Him that sat upon the horse, and against His army. And the beast was taken, and with him the false prophet that wrought the signs in his sight, wherewith he deceived them that had received the mark of the beast, and them that worshipped his image: they twain were cast alive into the lake of fire that burneth with brimstone: and the rest were killed with the sword of Him that sat upon the horse, even the sword which came forth out of His mouth: and all the birds were filled with their flesh" (Rev. 19. 11-21). Ezekiel similarly describes the scene in his prophecy in chapter 30. 17-21.

Thus it is that the climax of the world's rebellion against God is to meet its doom. This is the manner of the overthrow of the ten-kingdomed empire, the fourth of Daniel's visions. Accordingly, what we have now read from Revelation 19 is identical with (1) the falling of the stone upon the feet of the image in Nebuchadnezzar's vision, the annihilation of all Gentile government (Dan. 2. 45); (2) the consuming of the dominion of the fourth beast in Daniel's subsequent vision (Dan. 7. 26); (3) the pouring out of God's wrath upon the Antichrist, the desolator (Dan. 9. 27); and (4) the coming of the Son of Man on the clouds of Heaven with power and great glory (Matt. 24. 30). The great emperor, the man of sin, is to be crushed by the Lord Jesus, "with the breath of His mouth," and brought to nought "by the manifestation of His coming" (2 Thess. 2. 8).

Now this "manifestation of His coming" is, to transliterate the Greek words,

The Epiphany of His Parousia.

An epiphany is, literally, the 'shining forth' of that which has been hidden; and the word Parousia is, literally, 'presence' (see margin of R.V. and Phil. 2. 12). This latter word is used of the coming of Christ to the air for His saints, 'to receive them unto Himself,' and of their consequent presence with Him (1 Thess. 2. 19). They are thus to be "ever with the Lord" (1 Thess. 4. 17), and with Him they will come when He descends at His revelation "from Heaven with the angels of His power in flaming fire, rendering vengeance to them that know not God, and to them that obey not the Gospel of our Lord Jesus" (2 Thess. 1. 7, 8). The sudden bursting forth of His glory thus "to execute judgment" (Jude 15) will be the 'Epiphany, or shining forth, of His Parousia,' and by it the Man of Sin is to be brought to nought and his empire demolished. He and his false prophet will be "cast alive into the lake of fire," and his armies will perish (Rev. 19. 20, 21).

This is to be the issue of the world's attempts to establish a millennium of its own by schemes of federation and amalgamation. This is the upshot of its fancied progress and improvement without God and His Christ.

We must now see what other Scriptures have to say concerning this scene. The instrument which the Lord uses for the destruction of His foes is a sword which proceeds out of His mouth; the destruction is described as the treading of the winepress.

The Voice of the Lord.

First, as to the instrument. The sword is symbolic of the utterance of the Lord's voice. No material instrument is needed, a word is enough. This is clear from many passages. In the second Psalm the overthrow of the foe is thus described: "Then shall He speak unto them in His wrath, and vex them in His sore displeasure" (v. 5). Joel prophesies of the same event: "The sun and the moon are darkened, and the stars withdraw their shining: and the Lord uttereth His voice before His army; for His camp is very great; for He is strong that executeth His word: for the day of the Lord is great and very terrible; and who can abide it?" (Joel 2. 10, 11; and see 3. 16. With this compare Isa. 11. 4 and 30. 30-33.) The same voice of judgment is implied in Paul's prediction of the doom of the lawless one, that "the Lord Jesus will slay him with the breath of His mouth" (2 Thess. 2. 8). In the same connection we are doubtless to read Psalm 29, the Psalm which describes the terrible majesty and effect of the voice of the Lord.

We must presently dwell more fully upon this Psalm in order to observe its application to the circumstances under consideration, and its connection with the passages which describe the judgment of the foe as

The Treading of the Winepress.

These passages are Isaiah 63. 1-6; Joel 9. 16; Revelation 14. 17-20, and the one already quoted in Revelation 19. It is observable, too, that in the first of these the voice of the Lord is mentioned again, for the Deliverer describes Himself as "I that speak in righteousness."

We shall first refer to Revelation 14. 17-20. Two angels appear coming forth, the one from the temple in Heaven with a sickle in his hand, the other from the altar. The latter calls to the one with the sickle to gather "the clusters of the vine of the earth," symbolic of the Man of Sin and his gathered armies. The angel then casts his sickle into the earth, gathers the vintage, and casts it into the winepress of the wrath of God. The winepress is "trodden without the city," and "there came out blood from the winepress, even unto the bridles of the horses, as far as a thousand and six hundred furlongs" (i.e., 200 miles). The great emperor and his prophet, and their vast forces, will thus be gathered in dense battle array throughout the length of Palestine, Jerusalem being their objective. Joel calls the scene of the battle "the Valley of Decision." "Come, tread ye," says the prophet, "for the winepress is full, the fats overflow; for their wickedness is great. Multitudes, multitudes in the valley of decision! for the day of the Lord is near in the valley of decision" (Joel 3. 13, 14). The multitudes are the forces of the Man of Sin.

The first six verses of Isaiah 63 narrate in the form of a dialogue

The Overthrow of the Man of Sin

and his forces. The dialogue is between Messiah the Deliverer and the Jews. Having just overthrown the foe in the treading of the winepress, and the armies of the Empire being destroyed throughout the battle line from the north of the land to the south, the Messiah, in the fruits of His victory, reveals Himself to His astonished earthly people. In wondering admiration they exclaim: "Who is this that cometh from Edom, with dyed garments from Bozrah? this that is glorious, marching in the greatness of His strength?" To this their Deliverer answers, "I that speak in righteousness, mighty to save." The significance of this is at once apparent to the reader who calls to mind the various passages mentioned above in reference to the voice of the Lord. "I that speak in righteousness"--this is the voice uttered before His army (Joel 2. 10), "the sword that proceedeth out of His mouth" (Rev. 19. 15); the "breath of His mouth," by which the Man of Sin is crushed (2 Thess. 2. 8), and the "voice" of Psalm 29.

The people, struck by the appearance of the Victor, next ask: "Wherefore art Thou red in Thine apparel, and Thy garments like him that treadeth in the winefat?" The language is doubtless symbolic. Messiah explains in reply how the threatening foes have been crushed: "I have trodden the winepress alone; and of the peoples there was no man with Me: yea, I trod them in Mine anger, and trampled them in My fury; and their lifeblood is sprinkled upon My garments, and I have stained all My raiment. For the day of vengeance was in Mine heart, and the year of My redeemed is come. And I looked, and there was none to help; and I wondered that there was none to uphold: therefore Mine own arm brought salvation unto Me; and My fury, it upheld Me. And I trod down the peoples in Mine anger, and made them drunk in My fury, and I poured out their lifeblood on the earth" (vv. 3-6). The words of a previous prophecy express the joyful recognition of the delivered nation: "And it shall be said in that day, Lo, this is our God; we have waited for Him, and He will save us: this is the Lord; we have waited for Him, we will be glad and rejoice in His salvation" (Isa. 25. 9).

Turning now to Psalm 29 we find

The Scene of Judgment

strikingly depicted; the very length of the battle line is indicated, in agreement with the later and clearer description in Revelation 20. 14. Indeed, the passages which foretell the events of this coming terrible day afford a remarkable illustration of the progressive character of the revelations of Scripture. The Psalm is divided into three parts: (1) The first three verses are a call to the saints in Heaven, the "sons of the mighty," to worship the Lord in view of the judgment He is just about to execute for the deliverance of His people the Jews, their land and their city. (2) The second part, verses 3-9, describes the actual judgment by means of "the voice of the Lord." The psalmist was doubtless thinking of a thunderstorm. The Spirit of God was giving prophetic utterance concerning a more terrible scene, and the geographical limitations of the Psalm are of prophetic import. The first place mentioned is Lebanon, in the north, with its mountain-spur Sirion (vv. 5, 6). The last place is the wilderness of Kadesh, in the south, the centre of which is Bozrah, in Edom (v. 8), a point of connection with Isaiah 63. 1. Now the distance from Sirion to Bozrah, in the wilderness of Kadesh, is 200 miles, and this is the 1600 furlongs of Revelation 14.20. Here, then, in one fell stroke of divine wrath the Man of Sin and his forces are overthrown, and the Jews are delivered. The later revelations of Scripture thus enable us to pass from the natural and physical setting of the Psalm to the veiled reality. Thus this portion of the Psalm is to be read in connection with the passage from Revelation 19 quoted above. (3) The last two verses describe the results of the conquest.

The Jews in their Extremity

were threatened with annihilation. But man's extremity is God's opportunity. The people now see their Deliverer in person, they "look on Him whom they pierced." They realise that their enemies were destroyed because "the Lord sat as King at the flood." And now "the Lord sitteth as King for ever." He whose right it is to reign has come to Zion. Hence the psalmist can next say: "The Lord will give strength unto His people; the Lord will bless His people with peace." Armageddon is over, the winepress of God's wrath has been trodden, and the war against the Lamb is ended. Psalm 30 follows on with the people's song of praise for deliverance.

The judgments of God in the earth will be accompanied by

Seismic Disturbances,

including "a great earthquake such as was not since there were men upon the earth," the overthrow of the cities of the nations, and the displacement of islands and mountains (Rev. 16. 18-21). Then doubtless will be fulfilled the prophecy of Zechariah, that in the day when the Lord goes forth to fight against the nations that are gathered against Jerusalem, His feet will stand upon the Mount of Olives, and the mountain will be divided, leaving a very great valley east of the city (Zech. 14. 1-5).

The Everlasting Kingdom.

In this tremendous intervention in the affairs of the world for the termination of Gentile dominion the Son of God will be accompanied by all His saints. He will come "to be glorified in His saints, and to be marvelled at in all them that believed" (2 Thess. 1. 10). So from earliest times Enoch had prophesied: "Behold, the Lord came with His holy myriads, to execute judgment upon all" (Jude 14, 15, margin). And Zechariah: "The Lord my God shall come, and all the saints with Thee" (14. 5). They are to take an active part in the inauguration of His Kingdom, and in its government. For "the saints of the Most High shall receive the Kingdom, and possess the Kingdom for ever, even for ever and ever" (Dan. 7. 18). "The Kingdom and the dominion, and the greatness of the Kingdoms under the whole Heaven, shall be given to the people of the saints of the Most High" (v. 27).

Then shall the Lord "be King over all the earth" (Zech. 14. 9). God's claims will be vindicated. His Christ will reign as King of Righteousness, and King of Peace, the centre of His government being the very place where once He was despised and rejected, and men cast Him out and crucified Him. Of the increase of His government and of peace there shall be no end, upon the throne of David, and upon His Kingdom, to establish it, and to uphold it with judgment and with righteousness from henceforth even for ever. The zeal of the Lord of hosts shall perform this (Isa. 9. 7). His saints "shall be priests of God and of Christ, and shall reign with Him a thousand years" (Rev. 20. 6). Then will be fulfilled the words of the Lord, "I am returned unto Zion, and will dwell in the midst of Jerusalem: and Jerusalem shall be called the city of truth; and the mountain of the Lord of hosts the holy mountain" (Zech. 8. 3). The days of Israel's mourning will be ended, the nation will be a "crown of beauty in the hand of the Lord, and a royal diadem in the hand of her God," and Jerusalem will be a praise in the earth (Isa. 60. 30; 62. 3, 7). "The Heavens shall rejoice and the earth be glad," and "the earth shall be full of the knowledge of the Lord, as the waters cover the sea" (Psa. 96. 11; Isa. 11. 9). According to God's Eternal Counsel the despised Nazarene will yet be manifested and acknowledged by all as King of Kings and Lord of Lords.

"To Him be glory for ever and ever,

AMEN."

Made in the USA
Las Vegas, NV
26 August 2021